YOUR SEXUAL HEALTH™

HPV AND
GENITAL WARTS

ERIN STALEY

ROSEN
PUBLISHING®

New York

Published in 2016 by The Rosen Publishing Group, Inc.
29 East 21st Street, New York, NY 10010

Copyright © 2016 by The Rosen Publishing Group, Inc.

First Edition

Library of Congress Cataloging-in-Publication Data

Staley, Erin.
HPV and genital warts/Erin Staley.
    pages cm.— (Your sexual health)
Includes bibliographical references and index.
Audience: Grades 7–12.
ISBN 978-1-4994-6078-0 (library bound) — ISBN 978-1-4994-6079-7 (pbk.) — ISBN 978-1-4994-6080-3 (6-pack)
1. Human papillomaviruses—Popular works. 2. Genital warts—Popular works. I. Title.
QR406.S73 2016
614.5'47—dc23

                                                                    2014044515

Manufactured in the United States of America

CONTENTS

INTRODUCTION

Human papillomavirus (also called HPV) is a sexually transmitted infection (STI) that has received a lot of attention in the media in recent years. It has often been painted as a condition that affects only females, but the truth is that HPV affects males as well. Known as the "silent killer," HPV is noted by the Centers for Disease Control and Prevention (CDC) to be the most common of all STIs. In March 2014, the CDC estimated that nearly seventy-nine million Americans were already infected with HPV and that about fourteen million more become infected each year. Many of these people could be your family members, friends, neighbors, community leaders, teachers, boyfriends, or girlfriends. Most often, you cannot detect the presence of HPV in a person by their external appearance.

HPV is highly contagious. In fact, most sexually active males and females will get at least one type of HPV at some point in their lives. As scary as that may sound, the reality of living with HPV

If you are diagnosed with HPV, don't worry. You can still lead a normal, healthy life if you get the right treatment and know your facts.

isn't always so frightening. Most cases of HPV are harmless and will not interfere with your ability to lead a happy, healthy life. Usually, teens and adults with a healthy immune system dissolve the virus, sometimes without even knowing that they had it in the first place. But this doesn't mean you get a free-for-all pass when it comes to your sexual health. Why not? There are some cases of HPV that cause short-term or long-term discomfort, pain, and even more serious health issues. HPV can be a serious condition, so it is important to know how to protect yourself.

The best way to protect yourself against HPV or any STI is to know the facts. Here, you will learn about the virus, which strains of HPV could affect you, and how certain strains of HPV can lead to genital warts and cancer if not detected early enough. You will discover what to watch out for, what safety precautions you can take, and what treatments could be helpful depending on your diagnosis. Furthermore, you will find the hard facts and figures concerning HPV. And perhaps most important, you'll receive trusted advice on how to seek treatment and follow up with doctors to stay healthy.

The best way to be responsible for your sexual health is to educate yourself and debunk the myths surrounding HPV and genital warts. Know the right questions to ask your doctor and how to take care of your body. By educating yourself, you will be better equipped to make sound decisions regarding your sexual health. You'll also be able to share reliable information with your friends who may be too embarrassed to seek help.

CHAPTER ONE

In the Know: HPV

According to estimates by the CDC, "about 14 million people, including teens, become infected with HPV each year." HPV is one of the most contagious—and therefore most common—sexually transmitted infections. While an HPV infection itself can, in many cases, be harmless, an undetected or untreated HPV infection can put a person at risk for such diseases as genital warts and cancer. Furthermore, the CDC states, "Every year, approximately 17,600 women and 9,300 men are affected by cancers caused by HPV." The American Social Health Association estimates that three-fourths of sexually active people between ages fifteen and forty-nine have been infected with HPV at some point in their lives. That's why it is important to be educated on safe-sex practices so that you can live a long, happy, and healthy life.

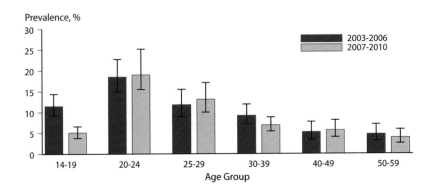

Prevalence, %

Legend: 2003-2006 / 2007-2010

Age Group: 14-19, 20-24, 25-29, 30-39, 40-49, 50-59

NOTE: Error bars indicate 95% confidence interval.
SOURCE: Markowitz LE, Hariri S, Lin C, Dunne EF, Steinau M, McQuillan G, et al. Reduction in human papillomavirus (HPV) prevalence among young women following HPV vaccine introduction in the United States, National Health and Nutrition Examination Surveys, 2003–2010. J Infect Dis. 2013;208(3):385–93.

This CDC chart shows the prevalence of the most common types of human papillomavirus among women aged fourteen to fifty-nine, sorted by age group and time period. The time periods are divided at the year of the introduction of the HPV vaccine for teenage girls in the United States.

HPV BASICS: AN ALL-INCLUSIVE VIRUS

To get an understanding of what HPV really is, let's start with its name. HPV stands for human papillomavirus. Human papillomavirus is a small, double-stranded DNA virus that lives in the epithelial cells of the skin's surface. A virus is a microorganism that invades living cells of a person or animal in order to grow, reproduce, and spread. Viruses, in general, are responsible for a wide range of illnesses and diseases, ranging from the common cold and herpes simplex to hepatitis and human immunodeficiency virus (HIV), which can cause acquired immunodeficiency syndrome (AIDS). Certain strains of human papillomavirus can cause cancer or genital warts (condyloma acuminata). In fact, *papilloma* is the Latin word for "warts."

HPV can affect anybody. It doesn't care who you are, where you live, what kind of social status you have, or what your sexual orientation may be. Any oral sex, genital-to-genital, or genital-to-anal contact with partners of the same or opposite sex has the potential to expose you to HPV if one partner is affected. HPV is spread through contact with infected mucous

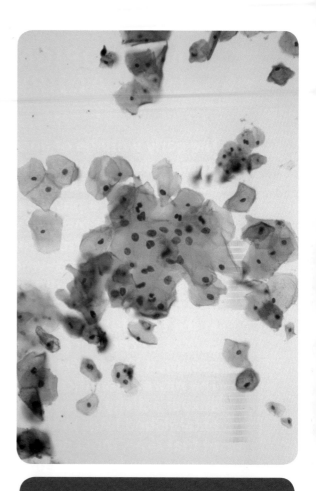

Human papillomavirus is the scientific name for the virus commonly called HPV. This microscopic view shows the virus, which lives inside cells on the skin's surface.

A HISTORICAL LOOK AT HPV

The early writings of ancient Greek and Roman civilizations detailed the discovery of genital lesions that looked similar to genital warts. In 1842, a physician in Florence, Italy, discovered that married women and prostitutes were dying from cervical cancer. However, local nuns–who did not engage in any sexual activity–did not have the same growths. Science was not advanced enough at the time for the physician to determine the causes of cervical cancer. (He incorrectly assumed that it was the use of tight corsets.) The more scientifically sound theory linking sexual activity to cervical cancer became established later in the 1960s. Nevertheless, at that time, most scientists believed cervical cancer was linked to herpes and not HPV.

In the 1980s, the most important research would be carried out to discover that there was indeed a link between HPV and cervical cancer. A German doctor named Harald zur Hausen found the DNA of human papillomavirus in cervical cancer cells. In the 1990s, studies detailed a consistent link between HPV and cervical cancer. Zur Hausen's work led to the 2006 development of an HPV vaccine called Gardasil. For his work, zur Hausen was awarded the Nobel Prize in Medicine in 2008.

membranes, bodily fluids, and genital skin. It is highly contagious, so somebody who does not have an active sex life can still contract HPV from a single sexual encounter—even his or her first. It is important to understand that even without sexual penetration, HPV can be transmitted from external contact. In fact, many young adults think that there is a safety zone where they can engage in sexual activity without penetration and avoid potential consequences. This is generally not true or safe, especially in the case of HPV. This virus is highly contagious.

THE MANY STRAINS OF HPV

Over one hundred strains of HPV have been identified. These have been scientifically categorized by numbers. While most HPV strains are harmless—causing warts on the hands and feet—there are forty that are not so innocent. They are particularly drawn to moist, mucousy areas of the body, such as the mouth, throat, vagina, vulva, cervix, penis, and anus. Low-risk HPV strains, such as 6 and 11, cause condyloma acuminata which are known as genital warts. Low-risk HPV strains also cause abnormal cervical cells and laryngeal papillomas (warts in the larynx). High-risk HPV strains, such as 16, 18, 31, 33, 35, 39, 45, 51, 52, 56, 58, 59, 68, 69, 73, and 82, can lead to cancer if not detected early enough.

The molecular model of HPV is shown above. The virus is highly contagious, and certain strands cause warts to appear on the skin or genitals. Other strands can cause cancer.

STAY IN THE KNOW

Very often an infected person may not show signs or symptoms of HPV. The virus remains in the body without indication. Thankfully, a healthy immune system usually suppresses HPV naturally. However, this process could take between eight and thirteen months. This wait time, during which a person may be infected but completely unaware of his or her infection, makes it easy to spread HPV to others. According to the nonprofit health

HPV:
FACTS AND FIGURES

Facts and figures are an effective way to highlight the effects that HPV has on individuals and communities at large. Worldwide health organizations keep track of HPV statistics in order to educate and protect the public. One such group is the Henry J. Kaiser Family Foundation. In September 2014, it published the following findings:

HPV is related to almost 100% of cervical cancer cases, with two strains (16 and 18) related to approximately 70% of cervical cancer cases. While cervical cancer is the main concern with HPV, the infection affects both women and men and is also known to cause oral, anal, vulvar, vaginal and penile cancers, as well as genital warts.

Cervical cancer affects only women, because men do not have cervixes. Nevertheless, HPV-related cancers can develop in men as well. Nearly 12,000 cases of throat (oropharyngeal) cancer occur in the United States each year. Two-thirds of these are linked to an oral HPV infection. Even though cervical cancer affects only women, occurrences of throat cancer are high enough among men (6.2 cases for every

100,000 people) that it follows cervical cancer as the second most common HPV-related cancer.

In terms of cervical cancer rates worldwide, the foundation's report stated, "In 2008, over 529,000 new cases of cervical cancer and 275,000 deaths attributed to cervical cancer occurred worldwide, with 86% of the cases in developing countries." Cervical cancer is usually treatable when detected early through routine screenings.

care organization Planned Parenthood, it is impossible for a sexually active individual who has had multiple partners to know when or from whom he or she contracted HPV. That is why it's more important than ever to stay vigilant about your sexual health. Understanding prevention and safer sex practices is the first step. Furthermore, it is important to be able to recognize noticeable symptoms and take advantage of annual screenings.

CHAPTER TWO

Genital Warts

Television shows, movies, popular music, websites, magazines, and advertisements often glamorize sex as something passionate, elegant, and even exotic. And sure, sex can be all those things and more, but media outlets often fail to mention the risks involved in engaging in sexual activity. An unwanted pregnancy or STI can seriously jeopardize the physical and emotional well-being of a young person. In fact, teens who aren't in the know regarding safe-sex practices could end up altering their futures forever.

When it comes to sexual health, the more knowledge that somebody has, the more empowered that person will feel with his or her decisions. There is a great deal of misinformation surrounding such topics as menstruation, masturbation, virginity, pregnancy, contraception, and STIs. While health classes in school or at-home conversations with parents or older siblings can answer a great deal of questions,

Educators and health care providers work together to provide students with detailed information on HPV. They raise awareness regarding the causes, symptoms, treatments, and methods of prevention.

these discussions can sometimes be difficult or embarrassing, and not every question is answered. Because ignorance is not a good enough reason to risk your health or future, it is important to tap into educational resources to fill in any informational gaps.

GENITAL WARTS 101

All warts are caused by a type of HPV. These include common warts, which are found on the hands; plantar warts, which are found on the bottom of the feet; and genital warts, which are found on the vagina, vulva, penis, rectum, scrotum, and anus. Warts are spread by physical contact—oral, genital-to-genital, or genital-to-anus—with a carrier. It can also be transmitted by reinfecting yourself, touching one's infected genitals with your fingers, then another's, or by sharing contaminated sex toys. However, HPV is not spread through hugs, handshakes, touching doorknobs, or other common surfaces, or sharing a bathroom, shower, hot tub, or swimming pool.

Genital warts come in a variety of shapes and sizes. They are soft and flesh-colored, appearing as raised bumps with a rough, cauliflower-like top or as flat bumps with a smooth finish. Inside the wart cores are tiny clusters of blood vessels that supply blood and keep the wart alive. Warts can appear alone or in clusters. Sometimes it is easy to find warts on the body, especially if they are common or plantar warts.

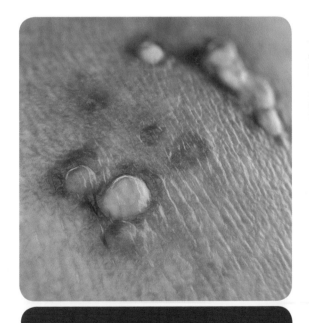

Genital warts may appear within weeks or months after contracting the virus. There may be an individual wart or a grouped outbreak, and genital warts may appear flat, raised, or in a cauliflower-like cluster.

However, it becomes more difficult if they are located in the folds or undersides of genitalia. That's why it is important to know how to conduct a self-examination.

WHAT YOU NEED TO KNOW ABOUT SELF-EXAMINATIONS

In general, a self-exam allows you to familiarize yourself with your body as a whole. You'll start to understand what is normal for you and what is abnormal, no matter if you are male or female. You might feel uncomfortable or a little funny at

There is no sure way to know when or how a person was infected with HPV. If you notice any unusual warts or have other questions about the virus, the first stop is to visit your doctor, who should be able to perform an examination for symptoms of the virus.

first, but becoming familiar with your own body will help you get over feelings of being self-conscious and help you feel empowered.

SELF-EXAMINATIONS FOR FEMALES

If you're a female, you will need a flashlight, a hand-held mirror, and some privacy. Find a comfortable bed or sofa with cushy pillows on which to lean. Put your knees up and open your legs. Shine the flashlight directly on the vulva or on the mirror itself. This will light up the entire area. First, examine the skin under any pubic hair. Then, separate the labia majora and labia minora—the inner and outer labia lips, or flaps that protect the vagina. You may notice that the skin comes in pink, purple, red, or brown hues and may appear to be splotchy, smooth, or uneven. This is normal. A little odor—musty or sweaty—and the presence of mucus are also normal. But be sure to consult a doctor if the mucus is green, gray, dark yellow, or white with a strong odor and a cottage cheese–like discharge. This could be an indication of a yeast infection or an STI. Use your fingers to feel around the vulva, paying close attention to any rough skin or bumps. After examining the vulva, take a close look at the anogenital skin (the skin around the genitals and anus) as well as the skin on your inner thighs. If any warts, lesions, blisters, sores, bumps, or white patches are present, consult your doctor. Once you've completed your self-exam, be sure to thoroughly wash your hands. Wipe down the flashlight, mirror, and any other tool you used with rubbing alcohol or a disinfectant solution.

SELF-EXAMINATIONS FOR MALES

If you're a male, you'll need the same tools to conduct a self-exam: a hand-held mirror and a flashlight. Find a private location and inspect the entire penis. If you are uncircumcised, be sure to pull back the foreskin and inspect the head of your penis. If you do not see any warts, lesions, blisters, sores, bumps, or white patches, then move on to the underside of your penis as well as the scrotum and the anus. Don't forget to check the skin underneath any pubic hair.

HOW OFTEN SHOULD I CHECK?

Both sexes should remember that HPV can live in the body for long periods of time. In general, genital warts appear within three weeks to six months after a sexual encounter with an infected partner, regardless of whether or not he or she develops any symptoms. Bear in mind, however, that it could take longer than six months. That is why repeating the self-exam on a regular basis can bring you greater peace of mind. Also keep in mind, however, that self-exams are not a substitute for regular HPV screenings by medical professionals.

MYTHS AND FACTS

MYTH

I've never had penetrative sex with a partner. I couldn't have contracted HPV.

FACT

Because HPV is transmitted through skin-on-skin contact, people who've never had sexual intercourse can still contract the virus. HPV-infected partners tend to "shed" the virus from their genital region. If your genitals, fingers, or mouth come in contact with "shed" cells, you could contract HPV, regardless of whether or not penetration occurred.

MYTH

I always use condoms, so I'm not at risk for genital warts.

FACT

Condoms are especially effective when it comes to preventing the exchange of bodily fluids. This means that they can significantly lower your risk of pregnancy and STIs. They do not, however, cover the entire genital area. A person could still contract HPV despite using a condom during every sexual encounter. This will be discussed in more depth in a later section.

MYTH

If I get HPV, I won't be able to have sex ever again.

FACT

This myth is entirely false. A person with HPV can enjoy a healthy sex life but may have to practice safe sex with every encounter—regardless of whether or not symptoms are apparent. However, if genital warts are present, it is safer to avoid oral, genital-to-genital, and genital-to-anal sexual activity entirely until the warts are removed.

CHAPTER THREE

HPV Prevention

Because genital warts and certain cancers are caused by an HPV infection, it is logical to first understand how HPV is contracted. After all, the smartest way for a person to protect him- or herself against HPV and other STIs is to use safe, preventative measures. Building life-long sexual health skills is the first step to keeping oneself in tip-top emotional, mental, and physical shape.

GOT SKILLS?

Communicating with your parents and partners about personal topics can be awkward and a little scary. Nonetheless, it's one of the best skills you can develop on your journey to becoming a well-adjusted, responsible adult. To do it right takes honesty—first with yourself and then with others. Other trusted adults, such as guidance counselors, older siblings, and teachers, can also provide support and guidance in making smart decisions when it comes to sexual activity and sexual health.

Decision making is another vital skill. Being responsible with your sexual health means you will have to be able to take in all options and then decide what works best for you and your needs. It could take time to consider your values and weigh the pros and cons. Most important, you should think through and decide if having sex is something you really want to do right now. The decision should be your own, and you should never let yourself be pressured to satisfy someone else's wants.

BUILDING HONEST, OPEN RELATIONSHIPS

With communication and decision-making skills in hand, the next step is to build honest, open relationships. A big part of this is being wise about your partner selection. Choose someone whom you can trust with your emotional and physical well-being. Spend time getting to know one another, your likes and dislikes, and your personal goals—in both relationships and life in general.

Oftentimes, engaging in sexual activity early in a relationship can distract from developing real interests. However, at a certain point you may decide that you want to engage in sexual activity with this person. If so, discuss safe-sex options as well as how you would handle any consequences. Be honest with your partner about your sexual history, and ask him or her to be upfront, too. Then discuss the idea of sharing a mutually monogamous relationship—meaning that neither of you engage in sexual activity with other partners. Why is this important? Because the fewer sexual partners a person has, the less likely he or she will be to come into contact with HPV or other STIs.

While it may sound distrustful or pessimistic, do not count on others to be upfront about their sexual history. They may be ashamed, embarrassed, or tempted to think that they'll be judged. In addition, they may not know that they have HPV. Remember, it is difficult to determine whether your partner is already infected as many people do not develop symptoms, and in those who do, the symptoms may take time to develop. This is normal, but it is all the more reason to take care of your own sexual health. Err on the side of caution by providing your own protection and asking your partner to undergo a screening. If you're no longer with that partner and want to pursue other relationships, lower your risk of contracting HPV and other STIs by limiting your number of sexual partners and always using the safe sexual practices discussed here.

PREVENTION MATTERS

Abstinence is the only 100 percent effective way to ensure you will not contract HPV, as well as prevent any other STI or unwanted pregnancy. Abstinence means to refrain from any sexual contact, including vaginal, anal, and oral sex. Abstinence works as a full-proof method only when those practicing it are sexually inactive without exception. Despite the fact that it is the only foolproof method to avoid STIs and unwanted pregnancy, abstinence is not a realistic option for everyone. There are other safe sex options to consider.

HIS AND HERS CONDOMS

Maintaining your sexual health is a big responsibility. If you think there's a chance that you'll engage in or continue engaging in sexual activity, be sure to supply your own method of protection. Also, don't be afraid to ask your partner to use a form of protection. It could save both of your lives.

Condoms help prevent HPV and other STIs. They come in all shapes, textures, and even colors. The most

Although latex condoms can lower the chance of infection, they do not prevent an HPV infection altogether. The virus can infect areas that are not covered by a condom.

highly recommended type of condom for pregnancy and STI prevention is latex. However, for those with a latex allergy, there are latex-free condoms made from polyurethane and polyisoprene. While condoms, when used correctly, are highly effective at preventing unwanted pregnancies or transmission of many STIs, HPV can still infect areas of skin that are not covered by a condom.

Most people are more familiar with male condoms, but female condoms are also effective when it comes to having safe sex. Female condoms are inserted into the vagina and primarily prevent against pregnancy and certain STIs. However, female condoms work only for genital-to-genital penetration. Furthermore, external contact with infected male or female genitalia can expose you to HPV and other STIs.

Mouth-to-genital contact can also result in the transmission of HPV. When engaging in oral sex with female genitalia, use a latex dental dam, an open condom cut lengthwise, or a sheet of plastic wrap. These are also effective when engaging in mouth-to-anal contact. Whichever type of condom you use—male or female—be sure to use them from start to finish with every sexual encounter. Follow all of the instructions on the packaging in order to lower the risk of unwanted pregnancy and STI transmission. Finally, never recycle a used condom.

HPV VACCINES: EASY AS 1-2-3

Vaccines are another important means of preventing HPV. Vaccines introduce very small doses of disease agents to the body, thereby stimulating the immune system to build up its defenses against the disease. They are used to prevent everything from polio to influenza. HPV vaccines work the same way. The CDC's "What Parents Should Know About HPV Vaccine Safety and Effectiveness" fact sheet states, "Data from clinical trials and ongoing research tell us that the protection provided by HPV vaccine is long-lasting." It furthermore explains, "Currently it is known that HPV vaccine works in the body for at least 10 years without becoming less effective."

Since the vaccine was recommended by the CDC in 2006, there has been a reported 56 percent reduction in HPV infections among adolescent girls in the United States. The HPV vaccine could help prevent the nearly 27,000 HPV-related cancers that annually affect men and women in the United States.

At the time of the CDC fact sheet, two HPV vaccines were widely available on the market in the United States: Gardasil and Cervarix. Both vaccines went through the approval process of the U.S. Food and Drug Administration (FDA) prior to their availability on the market. Administered in three doses over the course of twelve months, Gardasil protects females who have never been exposed to HPV, namely preteens between the ages of eleven and twelve years old. This age group has a higher immune response to the vaccine than any other. Gardasil targets specific strains of HPV—namely HPVs 6, 11, 16, and 18—that have been proven to cause cervical cancer as well as cancers of the throat, penis, and anus. It also protects against the HPV strains that cause most genital warts in both preteen males and females.

Cervarix is the second FDA-approved HPV vaccine. It targets HPV strains 16 and 18. Given in three doses over six months to females between the ages of eleven and twelve, Cervarix

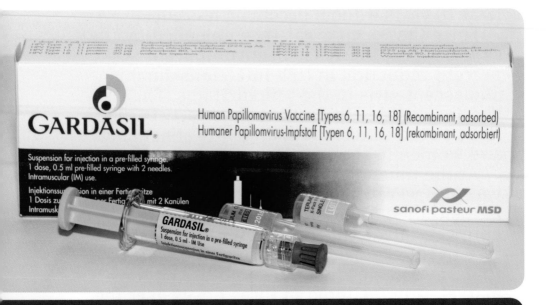

Gardasil has proven effective as a vaccine against strains of HPV that cause genital warts as well as cervical and penile cancers. Talk to a medical professional about this or any other vaccine options.

is over 90 percent effective in those who have already been exposed to HPV.

Parental consent must be given in order to receive the HPV vaccine. So-called catch-up vaccines are recommended for females between thirteen and twenty-six years old who did not get the full series or who did not complete the proper vaccine dosage at a younger age. Young men between the ages of thirteen and twenty-six are also encouraged to receive the vaccine. If too much time has passed between the administrations of vaccine doses, a patient does not need to start the series of vaccinations over from the beginning. However, the patient should still complete the series to maximize the benefits of the vaccine.

SIDE EFFECTS

Although the HPV vaccine is considered safe, it is still a medication. As with any medication, there are potential side effects that may occur along with the basic desired effect. In the case of the HPV vaccines, some patients—both male and female—experience mild to moderate reactions at the injection site. These can include pain, redness, swelling, and a mild to moderate fever of 100–102 degrees Fahrenheit (37.8–38.9 degrees Celsius). Some patients experience secondary side effects, such as headaches, dizziness, nausea, fainting spells, vision changes, and ringing in the ears. HPV

THE VACCINES FOR CHILDREN (VFC) PROGRAM

The price tag for vaccinations in the United States can be quite hefty. In the case of the HPV vaccine, the cost of the complete series can exceed five hundred dollars in the United States. Because many insurance companies won't always cover the costs of vaccination, the U.S. federal government formed the Vaccines for Children (VFC) program in 1993. This federally funded program offers no-cost vaccines for youth between nine and eighteen years of age who could not otherwise afford vaccination. The eligibility extends to those young people who are underinsured or uninsured, those who may be covered by Medicaid, and those who are of Native American or Alaskan Native descent. Once a young person is considered eligible for the VFC program, he or she can visit one of over 44,000 sites across the United States. These locations include hospitals as well as public and private health clinics. The CDC offers information regarding eligibility for the program.

vaccine side effects are temporary and should go away on their own. Allergic reactions, such as rashes or shortness of breath, are very rare. If you have reaction of any kind, tell your doctor or call 911 immediately.

SCHOOL-MANDATED HPV VACCINATIONS

Vaccination has been the subject of great debate. Those in favor of vaccines claim that vaccines are safe and historically have saved millions from such illnesses as polio, smallpox, diphtheria, rubella, and whooping cough. By late 2014, the CDC recommended ten vaccines for children under the age of six. Although there are no federal laws mandating vaccination, all fifty states require specific vaccinations before children can enroll in public schools. Those opposed to vaccinations claim that the immune system was designed to dissolve most infections naturally and that patients should not be forced to face the possible side effects of vaccines.

Some parents have moral objections to vaccines altogether, while others, who may be pro vaccination, simply do not agree with school mandates. Still yet, there are those who are concerned about the financial implications of making such vaccinations state laws. There are costs involved in funding such initiatives. Before deciding whether or not to require

Green Our Vaccines marchers on June 4, 2008, expressed concern over the possible connection between autism and heavy metals found in vaccines. They pushed for healthier vaccines in the medical industry.

HPV vaccinations in public schools, elected state officials must consider the local vaccine supply, the funds needed to implement such mandates, the burden on school employees to implement such laws, and the overall level of community support.

To date, twenty-five states and territories have passed legislation requiring HPV vaccination for public school enrollment. For families living in those states, parents are still able to object based on approved medical, religious, or philosophical exemptions. The details regarding these exemptions depend on the state in which a family lives.

CHAPTER FOUR

Screenings and Diagnosis

Because most people don't know whether or not they are infected with HPV, annual screenings are an important step toward taking charge of your sexual health. Screenings are medical examinations designed to detect the early stages of diseases such as HPV. They're the first line of defense against cervical cancer because they detect it in its most treatable stage. Although the techniques differ, screenings are available for both male and female patients.

MALE SCREENINGS

No matter what a young man's sexual orientation or previous status for HIV and other STIs may be, an HPV screening is an important part of his sexual health. In a screening, a doctor will visually inspect the penis, scrotum, and anus for the presence of genital warts and lesions. A vinegar wash may be used to make warts easier to see. While a visual screening for symptoms can be performed, there is no definitive test to determine the mere presence of asymptomatic HPV in males.

FEMALE SCREENINGS

A Greek doctor named Georgios Papanikolaou introduced what became known as the Pap test to the medical community in the 1940s. It was a time when cervical cancer was one of the highest causes of death among women in the United States. Papanikolaou started by studying the sex cycle of guinea pigs and then human vaginal cytology. Through his examinations, Dr. Papanikolaou used vaginal smears to detect abnormal cells on the cervix that could lead to cervical cancer. Today the Pap test is a standard cancer-screening test. Worldwide, it has greatly reduced the death rate for cervical cancer. Pap tests are usually performed by a gynecologist, doctor, physician's assistant, or

Georgios Papanikolaou developed the Pap test to detect premalignant conditions of cervical cancer in early stages. If cancerous conditions are discovered, treatment can minimize the development of cervical cancer.

nurse practitioner. Medical experts recommend screenings after age twenty-one, regardless of a patient's sexual activity. All women are encouraged to have routine Pap tests until they are sixty-five years old.

If you are a minor, then you can make the decision to have a parent stay with you during your gynecological appointment. Some girls want the comfort of having their mothers in the examination room, while others prefer the privacy to discuss confidential matters with their doctor. Be sure to express your preferences at the beginning of your appointment. A doctor, gynecologist, physician's assistant, or nurse practitioner will perform the exam, sometimes accompanied by another medical assistant.

At the time of the screening, a speculum, which is a type of medical device that allows doctors to examine orifices of the body, is inserted into the vagina. This gynecological tool holds the vaginal walls open. The physician will gently swipe the cervix with a specialized brush or long paddle, collecting cervical cells. These are then sent to

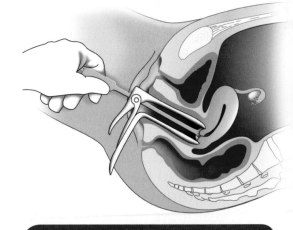

This illustration shows the insertion of a speculum. This tool holds the walls of the vagina open, allowing doctors to perform various medical procedures, including HPV screenings.

a lab where a pathologist will examine the cells under the microscope.

WHAT DO THE RESULTS OF MY PAP TEST MEAN?

If the cells collected during a Pap test are found to be normal, the test will come back negative. This is good news as it means the patient doesn't have any cell changes on her cervix. Still, she will need to continue having regular Pap tests in the future as new cell changes might eventually form on her cervix.

A Pap test could also come back as unclear, which means that the cervical cells appear to be abnormal. This abnormality may or may not be related to HPV; it could also simply be a result of other bodily changes such as an infection, pregnancy, or—in older women—menopause. An abnormal result means only that cell changes were detected on the cervix. It does not mean that a patient has cervical cancer. In the case of unclear results in a Pap test, a follow-up HPV test might be recommended to determine whether or not the cell changes are related to an HPV infection.

The cellular changes detected on a Pap test could be one of two grades: minor, which is low-grade, or serious, which is high-grade. Typically, minor cell changes resolve themselves without treatment while serious cell changes can develop

DO AS DIRECTED:
AN EXPERT INTERVIEW WITH PHYSICIAN ASSISTANT CAROL YAGHER

"There are many times when patients don't follow doctor's orders. This can slow down the healing process and cause conditions, such as genital warts, to spread," says Carol Yagher, a nationally certified physician assistant for over thirty-five years. She continues, "One particular patient of mine, a young woman in her early twenties, had a few genital warts on her labia. I sent her home with a prescription and treatment plan, but she ignored it and came back six months later with a growth the size of a grapefruit covering her entire vaginal area."

If genital warts aren't treated and are allowed to grow, they can form a blockage in the opening of the vagina, urethra, or anus. This can cause extreme discomfort and often makes it painful for the patient to urinate, ejaculate, or pass stool. At that point, Yagher says, "The only thing that can be done is to have the genital warts surgically removed. In the case of my patient, the procedure was long and painful, causing scars and reproductive issues."

"It's important for teens to think of their medical professionals as teammates in their health and well-being," Yagher explains. Always remember that the medical professionals whom you consult regarding your sexual health are your best allies in staying healthy and informed.

into cancer if not removed. In rare cases, women who receive an abnormal Pap test may have already developed cervical cancer. In that case, a doctor would run additional tests to be certain and follow up with the appropriate course of treatment.

If any abnormality is recognized, the test will be positive. But do not worry—false positives are very common! A doctor may simply recommend a Pap test repeat within three to six months. Otherwise, he or she might recommend an HPV test.

HPV TESTS FOR WOMEN

At present, there are two FDA-approved tests to follow up on abnormal results in a Pap test. These tests check the cervix for HPV—a common cause of abnormal cells that can sometimes lead to cervical cancer. The first test is the Hybrid Capture 2 HPV DNA test. This test is used to detect thirteen different high-risk viral strains of HPV. The second test is the Cervista HPV test. It is similar to the Hybrid Capture 2 test in that it checks for the same thirteen high-risk HPV strains. However, the Cervista test also checks for one more strain that has been found to cause cervical cancer.

If HPV is detected in either test, it does not necessarily mean that a patient has or will get cervical cancer. Remember that the majority of HPV infections clear up without special treatment or action. Unlike a Pap test, results from an HPV test will come back either negative or positive. A negative result means that the HPV strains that are associated with cervical cancer are not present in the patient. A positive result means that one of these HPV strains is detected. Keep in mind, however, that a positive HPV test result does not mean that a patient has already developed cervical cancer. Her doctor will advise her on how to proceed with treatments.

There are two FDA-approved HPV tests to check for the presence of the HPV virus. If the results of one of these tests are positive, then the presence of HPV strains associated with cervical cancer have been detected in the patient.

A DYNAMIC DUO FOR PREVENTING CERVICAL CANCER

Today, women thirty years of age or older are encouraged to have an HPV screening along with their routine Pap test. The rates of HPV are typically lower in women over thirty, but the occurrence of cervical cancer tends to increase. This is believed to result from a previous HPV infection that the body did not fight off on its own or that was not detected early enough. By combining the specific readings of a Pap test and the sensitivity of the HPV DNA test, a woman can get a highly effective screening for cancer and early symptoms that could lead to cancer. If both tests come back negative, a patient is at a low risk for developing cervical cancer. In that case, the frequency of screenings can be extended from once annually to once every three years.

OTHER SCREENINGS

For those who have had receptive anal sex, some medical professionals recommend anal pap smears to test anal cells for abnormalities. Also, if a sexually active patient experiences unexplained weight loss, an earache, a sore or hoarse throat, pain when swallowing, or enlarged lymph nodes, a medical professional may recommend a test for oropharyngeal (throat) cancer. A physical exam with scans, X-rays, and biopsies may also be performed. Consult with a medical health practitioner regarding any symptoms and necessary tests.

10 GREAT QUESTIONS
TO ASK AN EXPERT

If at any time you think you may have symptoms of HPV and genital warts, it is important to talk to your doctor as soon as possible. Below are some questions you might want to bring with you to your appointment.

1. Which vaccine(s) should I have?

2. How long am I protected after I've had a vaccine?

3. Can my partner also be vaccinated or tested for HPV?

4. How long do I have to wait for the results of a Pap test or an HPV test?

5. How should I expect to receive my test results?

6. Where can I get the financial help that I need to cover the costs of tests and treatment?

7. When should I come back for follow-up Pap tests, HPV tests, or treatment?

8. How will an infection and treatment affect my chances of someday getting pregnant and having healthy, HPV-free babies?

9. Can I still safely have sex if I've just been diagnosed with HPV?

10. Can I safely have sex despite having genital warts?

CHAPTER FIVE

Living with HPV

I f you've been diagnosed with HPV, you may feel devastated, confused, upset, or ashamed. You may want to cry, scream, or lash out at your partner. These initial reactions are normal, but it can't be said enough: HPV is incredibly common. Millions of people around the world have or will contract HPV in their lifetime, and for many, no life-threatening symptoms will develop. Statistically, you are not alone. Many of your friends, family, teachers, and the leaders in your community could be living with and treating an HPV infection, genital warts, or cancers caused by HPV.

PROCESSING A POSITIVE DIAGNOSIS

Should you receive a positive diagnosis for HPV, there are some things to do to process the information. First, collect yourself. Breathe. Ask questions. Take your time as you transition out of the doctor's office. Once you make it home, get comfortable. Put your to-do list on hold and focus on taking care of yourself. Don't be hard on yourself. Remember that having HPV doesn't mean that you're a bad person. You have nothing to feel guilty about or ashamed of.

In the days following a positive diagnosis, you may want to find a way to process your thoughts, feelings, and experiences. Some people do this by starting a journal or reaching out to a trusted family member, friend, or medical professional. You may even want to contact an HPV hotline. One example is the Centers for Disease Control and Prevention Voice Information System, which provides information about STIs, HIV, and tuberculosis. The toll-free number is 1-800-CDC-INFO (1-800-232-4636). There may also be HPV workshops and classes in your community. Sharing your experience and hearing from others who are going through the same thing will help alleviate the worry and give you practical ways to handle your treatment and well-being. Empowering yourself with education, resources, and support will help you get through this.

GIVING YOUR IMMUNE SYSTEM A LEG UP

While you're dealing with a positive diagnosis, take steps to keep your body in tip-top shape.

Remember that a healthy immune system can fight off HPV infections and flare-ups. You can boost your immune system by eating a healthy diet. This means filling your plate with power-packed fruits and vegetables, lean meats, and low-fat dairy products. Avoid high-fat and high-sugar processed foods. They tend to strip the body of much-needed vitamins and minerals. Also, steer clear of cigarettes, alcohol, and recreational drugs. These things slow down your immune system, making it more difficult to fight off an HPV infection.

One of the most important things you can do is also quite simple: don't forget to drink plenty of water! Water helps with digestion, the absorption of nutrients, the cushioning of organs, joint lubrication, regulating body temperature, and getting rid of waste. The Institute of Medicine's Food and Nutrition Board recommends that males between fourteen and eighteen years of age drink 112 fluid ounces

Help your immune system stay strong and ward off HPV infections naturally. Get plenty of rest and exercise, drink plenty of water, and load up your plate with healthy selections.

(just under 14 cups, or 3.3 liters) of water daily. Females in the same age group are encouraged to drink 78 fluid ounces (approximately 9.75 cups, or 2.3 liters) of water daily.

Another way to boost your immune system is to stay active. Regular physical activity has proven helpful in flushing unwanted elements out of the body, thus decreasing the chance of bacterial and viral infections. It can also rid the body of cancer-causing cells known as carcinogens through sweat and urine. Exercise circulates the body's defense cells—white blood cells—through the body more rapidly, detecting illnesses earlier than normal. This is thought to trigger a hormone release that warns immune cells of interfering bacteria or viruses. Exercise also slows down the release of stress hormones that normally increase the risk of illness.

Finally, you'll want to round out your immune-boosting regimen by getting plenty of rest. Timothy Morgenthaler, M.D., of Mayo Clinic, a highly ranked nonprofit health care organization, explains, "During sleep, your immune system releases proteins called cytokines, some of which help promote sleep. Certain cytokines need to increase when you have an infection or inflammation, or when you're under stress. Sleep deprivation may decrease production of these protective cytokines." He also explains that during periods where an individual does not get enough sleep, the antibodies and cells that he or she needs

PROFILE OF A CELEBRITY WHO FACED HPV AND GENITAL WARTS

The popularity that celebrities have often gives them a public voice to advocate for political change, a charitable cause, or even social awareness. In the case of Alexa Ray Joel–daughter of musician Billy Joel and supermodel Christie Brinkley–the star has been very open about having contracted HPV while in a relationship with her former boyfriend. In a 2011 interview for Sirius XM Radio's Jane Radio show, Joel commented: "I had [HPV]. But I mean, a lot of people get it..." She went on to say, "I wasn't angry with [my ex-boyfriend], because it's so common, and he wasn't cheating on me." She simply sought medical help and took care of her body accordingly.

Joel isn't the only celebrity to speak out

Founded in 2007, the Farrah Fawcett Foundation raises money to support cutting-edge cancer research, patient assistance for those burdened by treatment-related expenses, and HPV prevention programs.

on the issue of HPV. Another celebrity who committed her efforts and her finances to draw attention to HPV was Farrah Fawcett, the iconic *Charlie's Angels* actress from the 1970s. Fawcett was diagnosed with anal cancer in 2006. The following year, she started the Farrah Fawcett Foundation in order to find a cure for cancer. Her foundation specifically focused on furthering research into anal cancer as it was a lesser-known HPV-related cancer. Fawcett also wanted to help other patients pay for the expensive treatments and educate the public regarding protective measures. After the actress lost her battle with cancer in 2009, the Farrah Fawcett Foundation continued on with its mission.

to fight off infectious diseases are reduced. Effectively, sleep is essential in fighting off disease. According to Morgenthaler, teenagers need about nine or ten hours of sleep each night. With a healthy diet, plenty of water, physical activity, and rest, your body will be more likely to resist HPV infections.

SEEKING TREATMENT FOR GENITAL WARTS

By the time the CDC published its September 2014 fact sheets on HPV, there was still no definitive cure for the infection. However, several treatments had emerged that could limit the size, growth, and spread of genital warts. A patient with genital warts needs to team up with his or her physician to determine which treatment is right for him or her. This decision should take into consideration the size and location of the breakout as well as the cost and quantity of the treatment. If a treatment plan is approved, it'll focus on wart removal in order to prevent future outbreaks. Keep in mind that no treatment is 100 percent effective in fighting off HPV.

AT-HOME TREATMENTS

A popular first treatment option for wart removal is podofilox. Often known by its brand name Condylox, this topical solution or gel stops the growth of genital warts. It is for external genital use only, meaning it cannot be used internally in the vagina, urethra, or anus. After three consecutive days of twice daily application, the treated warts will eventually fall off. If not, the treatment can be continued for up to four weeks. Podofilox gel can be used at home and applied by the patient.

In addition to podofilox, there are several other prescriptions that can be applied at home. Veregen is a botanical drug made from green tea leaf extract. It's been proven to clear away genital warts for some patients within sixteen weeks. Aldara, an antiviral cream, lowers the chance of future outbreaks and speeds up the healing process. Desired results from Aldara should appear within sixteen weeks.

While many treatments can be applied by a patient him- or herself at home, they should always be done under a physician's guidance. Avoid all over-the-counter or "do-it-yourself" wart remedies. These often include duct tape and salicylic acid—which are designed for common warts on the hands and plantar warts on the feet. These treatments are not designed for the genital area and can cause serious damage or burning.

IN-OFFICE TREATMENTS

Other treatments are performed by a doctor, including the application of podophyllin resin. This solution is applied directly to the lesions. After several hours, it is washed off. Podophyllin treatments are repeated weekly until the genital warts have disappeared. Another doctor-applied weekly treatment is trichloroacetic acid (TCA) or bichloracetic acid (BCA) solution. Finally, a 5-fluorouracil epinephrine gel can be injected into the lesions until they are gone.

A more aggressive wart removal treatment is cryotherapy. This in-office procedure uses liquid nitrogen to freeze off a small spread of visible warts. The final step in removing genital warts is through surgery. There are

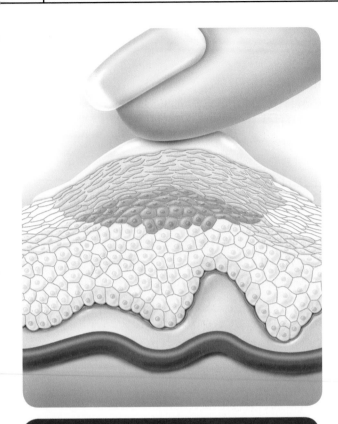

Depicted is a genital wart treatment known as an immunostimulant cream. When applied, the cream's primary ingredient stimulates the immune system to heal any warts on the surface of the skin.

three options for surgery: electrosurgery, curettage, and laser surgery. Electrosurgery uses a high-frequency current to burn off the wart while curettage uses a knife or spoon-shaped tool to cut off the wart. Laser surgery burns the wart off using an intense beam of light in smaller areas. The success of any of these three options depends on the patient and the number of warts present. Any treatment option should be chosen only after an in-depth discussion with a doctor or other health care professional.

Keep in mind that wart removal can be painful as the area around the genitals is extremely sensitive. Plus, you may experience scarring with electrosurgery, curettage, and laser surgery.

WHAT DO I DO AFTER TREATING GENITAL WARTS?

Wart removal does not eliminate an HPV infection altogether. You may still experience flare-ups or even spread the infection to future partners. But if you've had one treatment and warts return later, you can consult with your physician about another treatment option. Another important follow-up discussion should occur for female patients who are pregnant or thinking about having a baby. HPV-related complications are rare but could be passed on to a newborn child. Some prescription medications could also cause birth defects.

SEEKING TREATMENT FOR CANCER

Patients diagnosed with cancer due to an HPV infection should seek the guidance of a health care professional, who can discuss treatment options including surgery, external beam radiotherapy, and chemotherapy. With early detection, cancer is usually treatable. If a woman undergoes cervical cancer treatment, there is a possibility that she will not be able to have children later. Female patients should discuss this possibility with their doctor.

PREGNANCY AND HPV

Most pregnant women with HPV have natural deliveries and healthy children. If genital warts block the birth canal, a Caesarean section, or C-section, is recommended. If the newborn infant does contract HPV 6 or 11 during childbirth, it could develop warts in the throat that cause hoarseness and difficulty breathing. This is called recurrent respiratory papillomatosis (RRP). According to the CDC, RRP is rare with less than 2,000 children affected each year. Surgery is recommended for RRP and can be repeated if and when the warts reoccur. Doctors recommend that mothers-to-be undergo screenings, both before and after their pregnancy, to determine the best course of action for their deliveries.

SHARING THE NEWS

As noted earlier, HPV may take weeks, months, or even years after exposure to manifest symptoms or show up on a screening. If your test comes back positive for HPV, it is important to know two things. First, it is very difficult to determine when or from whom you contracted HPV. Second, it does not mean that either you or your partner has been unfaithful. With that being said, the next steps are to accept the news, work with your doctor, practice safe sex, and be open with your partner about your diagnosis. Assure him or her that HPV is extremely common. Share statistics about the number of people who are sexually active and then become exposed to the virus. No matter how embarrassing or nerve-racking it may feel, be honest from the start. Consider it a favor to your partner, helping him and her to make sound decisions regarding his or her own sexual health. Encourage your partner to visit a physician, all the while knowing that the virus may not show visible symptoms at the time of the screening.

In many cases, sexually active couples that have been together for a while will share an HPV infection, regardless of visible symptoms. Often their bodies will fight the infections off naturally and then "remember" that strain, likely becoming immune to it.

Even if you have fought off a previous HPV infection, continue to take safe-sex precautions as becoming immune to one HPV strain may not protect you from contracting others. And now that you've learned about HPV and genital warts, be sure to take care of yourself with healthy decisions and practices. Enjoy a happy and healthy life, and make the most of the knowledge you have and all available resources.

GLOSSARY

anogenital Relating to the genital organs and the anus.

Caesarean section Surgical incision of the walls of the abdomen and uterus for delivery of offspring.

cervical Of or relating to the cervix.

cervix The narrow lower or outer end of the uterus.

cytology A branch of biology dealing with the structure, function, multiplication, pathology, and life history of cells.

dental dam A type of rectangular sheet, usually made of latex rubber, used in dentistry.

epithelial cells Cells that cover a free surface or line a tube or cavity of an animal body.

gynecologist A specialist who works in the branch of medicine that deals with the diseases and routine physical care of the reproductive system of women.

larynx The upper part of the trachea that, in human beings and most mammals, contains the vocal cords.

lesion A change in the structure of a bodily organ or part due to injury or disease.

monogamous Describing a romantic or sexual relationship in which two partners are exclusively engaged with each other and no other partners.

nurse practitioner A registered nurse who, through advanced training, is qualified to assume some of the duties and responsibilities formerly assumed only by a physician.

over-the-counter Medication sold lawfully without a prescription.

pathologist A specialist in the path of science known as pathology, which interprets and diagnoses the causes and effects of disease in tissues and body fluids.

physician assistant A person certified to provide basic medical services usually under the supervision of a licensed physician.

smear A very small sample of skin or blood that is then usually examined with a microscope.

speculum A medical instrument inserted into a body passage to facilitate visual inspection.

topical Used on the external surface of the skin.

vulva The external part of the female genital organs.

FOR MORE INFORMATION

American Sexual Health Association (ASHA)
P.O. Box 13827
Research Triangle Park, NC 27709
(919) 361-8400
Website: http://www.ashasexualhealth.org
Since 1914, ASHA has been an authority for
    sexual health information in the United States.

Canadian Federation for Sexual Health (CFSH)
2197 Riverside Drive, Suite 403
Ottawa, ON K1H 7X3
Canada
(613) 241-4474
Website: http://www.cfsh.ca
The CFSH promotes sexual and reproductive
    health and rights in Canada.

Canadian Public Health Association (CPHA)
404-1525 Carling Avenue
Ottawa, ON K1Z 8R9
Canada
(613) 725-3769
Website: http://www.cpha.ca
Found in 1910, the CPHA advocates for the
    maintenance and improvement of both
    individual and community health.

Centers for Disease Control and Prevention (CDC)
1600 Clifton Road
Atlanta, GA 30333
(800) 232-4636 (1-800-CDC-INFO)
Website: http://www.cdc.gov

The CDC addresses global health issues, including disease, health threats, causes of death and disability, and refugee health.

The Henry J. Kaiser Family Foundation
2400 Sand Hill Road
Menlo Park, CA 94025
(650) 854-9400
Website: http://kff.org
As a nonprofit organization, the Kaiser Foundation provides facts, analysis, and reports for the government, the media, the health policy community, and the general public.

Planned Parenthood Federation of America
1110 Vermont Avenue NW, Suite 300
Washington, DC 20005
(202) 973-4800
Website: http://www.plannedparenthood.org
Planned Parenthood encourages women's health worldwide.

WEBSITES

Because of the changing nature of Internet links, Rosen Publishing has developed an online list of websites related to the subject of this book. This site is updated regularly. Please use this link to access the list:

http://www.rosenlinks.com/YSH/HPV

FOR FURTHER READING

Dizon, Don S., and Michael L. Krychman. *Questions & Answers About Human Papilloma Virus (HPV)*. Sudbury, MA: Jones and Bartlett Publishers, 2010.

Gowey, Brandie. *Your Cervix Just Has a Cold: The Truth About Abnormal Pap Smears and HPV*. New York, NY: Morgan James Publishing, 2014.

Handsfield, Hunter. *Color Atlas & Synopsis of Sexually Transmitted Diseases*. 3rd ed. New York, NY: The McGraw-Hill Companies, 2011.

Hasle, Nikol. *Sex: A Book for Teens: An Uncensored Guide to Your Body, Sex, and Safety*. San Francisco, CA: Orange Avenue Publishing, 2010.

Henderson, Elisabeth. *100 Questions You'd Never Ask Your Parents: Straight Answers to Teens' Questions About Sex, Sexuality, and Health*. New York, NY: Roaring Brook Press, 2013.

The National Cervical Cancer Coalition. *HPV & Cervical Cancer: Stories from Survivors and Supporters*. Research Triangle Park, NC: American Sexual Health Association, 2014.

Pardes, Bronwen. *Doing It Right: Making Smart, Safe, and Satisfying Choices About Sex*. New York, NY: Simon Pulse, 2013.

Roizen, Michael F., and Mehmet Oz. *The Owner's Manual for Teens: A Guide to a Healthy Body and Happy Life*. New York, NY: Free Press, 2011.

BIBLIOGRAPHY

American Cancer Society. "How Much Do the HPV Vaccines Cost? Are They Covered by Health Insurance Plans?" Retrieved August 23, 2014 (http://www.cancer.org).

American Sexual Health Association. "Ten Things to Know about HPV." Retrieved August 11, 2014 (http://www.ashasexualhealth.org/uploads/pdfs/10ThingsHPV.pdf).

Bringle, Jennifer. *Young Women and the HPV Vaccine*. New York, NY: The Rosen Publishing Group, 2012.

Centers for Disease Control and Prevention. "Genital HPV Infection - Fact Sheet." Retrieved August 2, 2014 (http://m.cdc.gov/en/HealthSafetyTopics/DiseasesConditions/STDs/genitalHPV_FS).

Centers for Disease Control and Prevention. "HPV Vaccine—Questions & Answers." Retrieved August 22, 2104 (http://www.cdc.gov/vaccines/vpd-vac/hpv/vac-faqs.htm).

Centers for Disease Control and Prevention. "Human Papillomavirus (HPV)." Retrieved August 2, 2014 (http://www.cdc.gov/hpv/prevention.html).

Centers for Disease Control and Prevention. "Human Papillomavirus: Epidemiology and Prevention of Vaccine-Preventable Diseases." The Pink Book: Course Textbook. 12th ed. 2012. Retrieved September 22, 2014 (http://www.cdc.gov/vaccines/pubs/pinkbook/hpv.html).

Centers for Disease Control and Prevention. "VFC Detailed Questions and Answers for Parents." Retrieved August 22, 2014 (http://www.cdc .gov/vaccines/programs/vfc/parents/qa -detailed.html).

Centers for Disease Control and Prevention. "What Parents Should Know About HPV Vaccine Safety and Effectiveness." 2014. Retrieved September 30, 2014 (http://www .cdc.gov/vaccines/who/teens/vaccines/ vaccine-safety.pdf).

Healthwise, Incorporated. "Genital Self-Examination—Topic Overview." Retrieved September 22, 2014 (http://www.webmd .com/sex/tc/genital-self-examination-topic -overview).

The Henry J. Kaiser Family Foundation. "The HPV Vaccine: Access and Use in the U.S." Retrieved September 22, 2014 (http://kff .org/womens-health-policy/fact-sheet/the -hpv-vaccine-access-and-use-in).

Knox, Richard. "HPV Vaccine: The Science Behind the Controversy." NPR, September 19, 2011. Retrieved August 19, 2014 (http:// www.npr.org/2011/09/19/140543977/hpv- vaccine-the-science-behind-the-controversy).

The Labia Library. "Are My Labia Normal?" Retrieved September 22, 2014 (http://www .labialibrary.org.au/your-labia/are-my-labia- normal).

MedicineNet. "Podofilox—topical solution, Condylox." 2014. Retrieved September

29, 2014 (http://www.medicinenet.com/podofilox-topical_solution/article.htm).

National Institute on Deafness and Other Communication Disorders (NIDCD). "Recurrent Respiratory Papillomatosis or Laryngeal Papillomatosis." Retrieved September 25, 2014 (http://www.nidcd.nih.gov/health/voice/pages/laryngeal.aspx).

Nilsen, Richard. "Famous People with HPV." Retrieved October 1, 2014 (http://www.livestrong.com/article/26370-famous-people-hpv).

Planned Parenthood. "Genital Warts." Retrieved September 22, 2014 (http://www.plannedparenthood.org).

Stöppler, Melissa Conrad, MD. "Sexually Transmitted Diseases (STDs in Women)." MedicineNet.com, 2014. Retrieved September 29, 2014 (http://www.medicinenet.com).

WebMD. "Abstinence vs. Sex Ed." Retrieved September 30, 2014 (http://www.webmd.com/parenting/features/abstinence-vs-sex-ed).

WebMD. "Information About the Human Papillomavirus (HPV)." Retrieved August 24, 2014 (http://www.webmd.com/sexual-conditions/hpv-genital-warts/hpv-virus-information-about-human-papillomavirus).

Yagher, Carol. Interview by Erin Staley. Indio, CA: October 5, 2014.

INDEX

ABOUT THE AUTHOR

After running a successful dance program for over a decade, Erin Staley took her stories from the stage to the page as a writer. Forever a student of the human condition, Erin has fostered a passion for the inner workings of the mind and body.

PHOTO CREDITS